Discovering Mission Nuestra Señora de la Soledad

BY ZACHARY ANDERSON

Cavendish Square

New York

Published in 2015 by Cavendish Square Publishing, LLC
243 5th Avenue, Suite 136, New York, NY 10016

Library of Congress Cataloging-in-Publication Data

Anderson, Zachary.
Discovering Mission Nuestra Señora de la Soledad / Zachary Anderson.
pages cm. — (California missions)
Includes index.
ISBN 978-1-62713-079-0 (hardcover) ISBN 978-1-62713-081-3 (ebook)
1. Nuestra Señora de la Soledad (Mission : Calif.)—History—Juvenile literature. 2. Spanish mission buildings—California—Soledad Region—History—Juvenile literature. 3. Esselen Indians—California—Soledad Region—History—Juvenile literature. 4. Franciscans—California—Soledad Region—History—Juvenile literature. 5. California—History—To 1846—Juvenile literature. I. Title.
F869.N8A54 2015
979.4'76—dc23
2014006066

Editorial Director: Dean Miller
Editor: Kristen Susienka
Copy Editor: Cynthia Roby
Art Director: Jeffrey Talbot
Designer: Douglas Brooks
Photo Researcher: J8 Media
Production Manager: Jennifer Ryder-Talbot
Production Editor: David McNamara

The photographs in this book are used by permission and through the courtesy of: Cover photo by Lordkinbote/File:Nuestra Senora del la Soledad chapel.jpg/Wikimedia Commons; Stock Connection/SuperStock, 1; Stephen Saks/Lonely Planet Images/Getty Images, 4; De Agostini/Getty Images, 7; Marilyn Angel Wynn/Nativestock/Getty Images, 8; Marilyn Angel Wynn/Nativestock/Getty Images, 10; © 2014 Pentacle Press, 12; Universal Images Group/SuperStock, 13; Antandrus/File:SanArdoOilfieldView.jpg/Wikimedia Commons, 15; Nheyob/File:Mission San Carlos Borromeo de Carmelo (Carmel, CA) - Mora Chapel, cenotaph – Fray Fermín Lasuén.jpg/Wikimedia Commons, 17; Bridgeman Art Gallery/Getty Images, 18; © Courtesy California Missions Resource Center (CMRC), 21; Bloomberg via Getty Images, 22; © Courtesy CMRC, 24; Tom Simondi/missiontour.org, 26; © Pentacle Press, 28; © North Wind/North Wind Picture Archives, 31; Edwin Deakin/File:Deakin NSS circa 1899.jpg/Wikimedia Commons, 32; © Robert Fried/Alamy, 34; Lordkinbote/File:Nuestra Senora del la Soledad chapel.jpg/Wikimedia Commons, 41.

Printed in the United States of America

CALIFORNIA
MISSIONS

Contents

Mission Nuestra Señora de la Soledad is part of the mission system built along California's coast in the 1700s and 1800s.

1
The Spanish in California

Thirty miles (48.2 km) southeast of Monterey and one mile (1.6 km) west of the Salinas River lies a beautiful land that was once the shared home of Spanish **friars** and Native Americans. Although their backgrounds and cultures differed greatly, the groups lived together, worked together, and made history together through the mission system, a series of religious buildings along California's coast. The Spanish, who built the structures, wanted to bring **Christianity** and Spanish ways to the Native Californians. Mission Nuestra Señora de la Soledad was one mission that played an interesting role in the history of California.

AN AGE OF EXPLORERS

The fifteenth and sixteenth centuries were times of great exploration throughout the world. European explorers were eager to discover new lands in search of great treasures, such as gold and spices, as well as new trade routes across the seas. Spain sent an Italian explorer, Christopher Columbus, on one such expedition. Columbus traveled the seas searching for a route between Europe and Asia. Instead he discovered the so-called New World (North America, South America, and Central America) in 1492. Spain then explored North America and its western coast. At this time, many people believed that a river ran through America from the Atlantic Ocean to the Pacific Ocean. If such a river existed, it would mean that sailors could reach Asia faster and bring back riches such as tea, silk, and spices to sell in Europe.

A NEW COUNTRY

In the years that followed, several important men increased the lands of the Spanish empire by claiming parts of the New World for Spain. First was Hernán Cortés, a soldier, who in 1519 traveled to the land known today as Mexico. In 1521, Cortés and his men conquered the great Aztec empire and claimed the Aztec lands for Spain, which they renamed New Spain. They established a government there under a **viceroy**.

In 1542, an explorer named Juan Rodríguez Cabrillo was the first European to see the coast of *Alta*, or upper, California from the sea. Along his journey, he found many Native people, but no riches. He also found no evidence of a river passage through North America. Sadly, Cabrillo died before he could return to New Spain, and his expedition was called a failure. However, many people today regard Cabrillo as the first European explorer of the California coast.

In 1602, Sebastián Vizcaíno was sent by New Spain's rulers to find harbors along Alta California's coast. While Vizcaíno did establish Monterey Bay, named after the viceroy of New Spain, and kept detailed maps, he did not find anything new. It was for this reason that Spain did not sail to California for the next 160 years.

2
The
Esselen People

When the Spanish arrived in Alta California, many different groups of indigenous, or Native, people were already living there. The groups that lived at Mission Nuestra Señora de la Soledad were from the Ohlone, Esselen, Yokut, and Salinan tribes. While the area around the mission did not have a large Native population, these groups were brought to the mission to live and work. Speaking different languages, the tribes had lived separately in different areas of California prior to the arrival of the Spanish. It is not known when the first indigenous people arrived in the

Many different Native groups came to live at the twenty-one missions.

California area, but some suggest that more than 10,000 years ago a group traveled across a bridge of land that once connected Siberia and Alaska, and then walked down to settle along the California coast. The main group of indigenous people living around the area where Mission Nuestra Señora de la Soledad was built was called the Esselen.

A WAY OF LIFE

The Esselen were, by population standards, a small group. It has been said that the tribe went extinct in the 1840s, but that is incorrect. There is even recent evidence that some Esselen escaped the missions entirely by retreating to the rugged Santa Lucia Mountain region. Unfortunately, no information on the structures they lived in remains, but it is thought they built rounded huts like other Native groups.

Music was important to many Native groups. Several tribes throughout California used an instrument known as a clapper stick, as seen here.

Like most groups in the Monterey area, the Esselen were hunters and gatherers, living off the land and animals that surrounded them. Acorns were the most important part of the tribe's diet, though they also gathered berries, nuts, grapes, mushrooms, and roots. The men of the tribe fished and hunted for animals such as salmon, deer, prairie dogs, elk, otters, and rabbits.

CLOTHES MADE BY HAND

Clothing varied depending on the region and the season. Usually, in the warmer months, the men and children of the tribe did not wear garments. The women wore skirts made of bark, grass, or hide. In colder climates, they wore capes or blankets made of animal hides. Rabbit fur or deer fur often was used, but otter fur was thought to be the warmest. Both men and women wore necklaces made of stones and shells. Women sometimes wore earrings.

CRAFTS

The women were well known for their skills in basket making. Baskets were used for many different tasks such as collecting food and cooking. Most baskets were so tightly woven that they could be used to store and transport water. Other crafts the Native people enjoyed included bow-and-arrow making and creating their own musical instruments. Music was especially important to the Native people, as it was a way of expressing themselves and their beliefs. Records show the Esselen did not use certain instruments made by other tribes, such as the hide drum. Instead they used a split "clapper" stick that was possibly made of elderberry.

RELIGIOUS BELIEFS

The clapper stick the Esselen used is still part of traditional Native music today.

The Esselen, like the other Native people brought to Nuestra Señora de la Soledad, believed that there were spirits all around them, and that everything had a spirit. Many tribes, including the Esselen, had religious healers, or **shamans**. Shamans were believed to be closer to the spirit world than other people. Tribes had different shamans for different tasks. A shaman was believed to be able to control the weather, cure sickness, or predict whether there would be a good harvest.

Each tribe had its own religion, language, and culture, but the arrival of the Spanish changed that forever. The effects of the mission system on the Native people still can be seen. Today many of their languages are no longer spoken and there are few full-blooded members of the tribes still living.

3
The
Mission System

After the Spanish decided to stop sailing to California in the 1600s, other countries, such as Russia and Britain, looked to settle the land. It was not until the 1760s that Spain's king, Carlos III, saw these countries as threats to his claim on California. He decided to send soldiers and friars to Alta California to establish *presidios*, or forts, and religious communities called missions. These communities had already been set up in *Baja*, or lower, California. King Carlos thought that if missions were also started in the Upper California region, he could better control the land and expand his empire. His plan was for the friars to use the missions to **convert** the Native people and make them into Spanish citizens by teaching them how to adopt the Spanish culture and language. The soldiers would help keep the missions, and the coast, safe.

THE SPANISH AND THE NATIVE PEOPLE

At the time of the first missions, many people in Europe believed that the indigenous Californians' culture was primitive. Today we know that the Native peoples' culture was different from the Spanish, but not bad by any means. The tribes living in California had their own interesting and successful cultures that had kept them productive and healthy for generations. The Spanish thought that they were helping the Native people by making them wear clothes, speak Spanish, and become Christians. However, in reality, the Spanish only damaged and changed the Native people by taking away their culture and traditions.

The friars, called *frays* in Spanish, wanted to convert the Native people because they wanted to spread their religion. In the Christian religion, it is believed that only Christians go to heaven

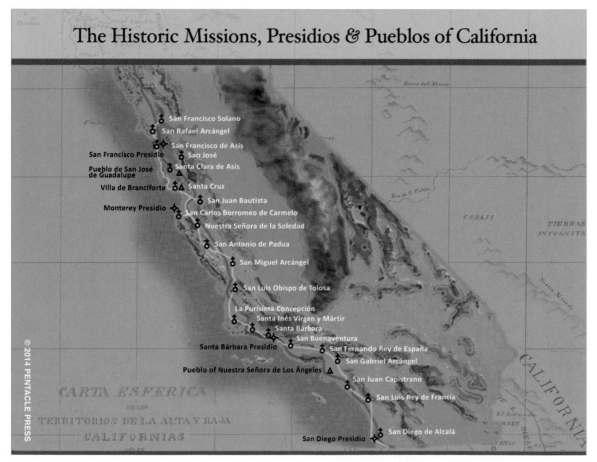

Spanish friars and soldiers started twenty-one missions and four presidios in California between 1769 and 1823.

Fray Junípero Serra was the first leader of the Alta California mission system.

after death. The friars thought it was their duty to teach other people about Christianity. A person who travels to other countries teaching people about Christianity and encouraging them to follow the teachings of Jesus Christ and the Bible is called a missionary. A Native person who lived at the mission and converted to Christianity was called a **neophyte**.

The Spanish enlisted fifty-five-year-old Fray Junípero Serra to found the first Alta California mission and establish others along the coast. He had come to Mexico City in 1749. In 1767, he was asked by the Spanish ruler to head the missions of Baja California. A year later, he became the first president of the Alta California missions. Under his reign he founded the first nine missions. Altogether there would be twenty-one missions founded between 1769 and 1823, all connected by a road called *El Camino Real*, meaning "The Royal Road."

4
Founding the Mission

Mission Nuestra Señora de la Soledad was the thirteenth of the Alta California missions. It was dedicated in October 1791, just a few months after Mission Santa Cruz was founded. Although founded amid the "Golden Age" of the California missions, it was one of the least successful, only having 687 inhabitants at its peak in 1804. However, the story of its founding is full of interesting and important figures and facts.

THE LONELY LAND

Several important elements were needed in order to find the right place to start a mission: a reliable source of water, good soil for farming, plenty of wood for building materials, and a Native population for the friars to convert. The lands around the coast of California had all of these things, though in varying amounts, as those at the mission discovered.

One of the first Spanish explorers to cross into the Salinas River Valley was Gaspár de Portolá in 1769. The Spanish government had tasked Portolá to find the port of Monterey, which Vizcaíno had claimed in 1602. Soldiers and Fray Juan Crespí, the military chaplain, or priest, who was on the lookout for new mission sites, joined Portolá. This expedition was divided: two groups, one led by Portolá, would go over land, while three other groups journeyed by sea. It was Spain's first attempt to reclaim the land of Alta California. During the journey, Portolá and his men found refuge in a harbor in San Diego, an area that Vizcaíno had passed on his expedition. They then ventured in search of the infamous Monterey Bay. Their journey took them to a valley near the Salinas River, which was a barren land with grasses and desert mixed with rolling hills. At first glance, it seemed to have everything required for a mission: land, water, and Native people. What Portolá did not know at the time was that this place grew unbearably hot in the summer and cold and damp in the winter. It also had a small Native population, which was not good for the friars who had come to convert people.

Mission Nuestra Señora de la Soledad was founded near the Salinas River, in an isolated and peaceful valley.

NAMING THE MISSION

There are several stories of how Mission Nuestra Señora de la Soledad got its name. First, in 1769, when Fray Juan Crespí and Gaspár de Portolá traveled through the Salinas River Valley, it is said that some of the Esselen came to see them there. However, the Spanish and the Native people could not understand one another's language. One of the Esselen was asked about the area, and he said something in his language that sounded like the Spanish word *soledad*, which means "lonely." The area did appear isolated and quiet. Another story occurs in 1771, when Fray Serra passed through the area. He met an Esselen woman along the way, and when he asked her name, she responded with what he thought was "Soledad."

Twenty years later, the mission was founded in the Alta California area and appropriately named Mission Nuestra Señora de la Soledad for the Virgin Mary, who sometimes is called Our Lady of Solitude. It is often referred to as Mission Soledad.

THE MISSION BEGINS

In 1791, Fray Fermín Francisco de Lasuén, who took over leading the missions after Fray Serra passed away in 1784, decided that a new mission was needed to connect Mission San Antonio de Padua and Mission San Carlos Borroméo del Río Carmelo. The mission would be halfway between the two, and it would only take a day's walk to travel from the new mission to either San Carlos or San Antonio.

Soon after the decision had been made, Fray Lasuén wrote to the friars at Mission San Carlos Borroméo. He told them that he was going to found a mission in the valley near the Salinas River and asked them to send some neophytes there to prepare for his arrival. A group of neophytes and soldiers left Mission San Carlos Borroméo in September, carrying supplies for the new mission.

Fray Fermín Francisco de Lasuén was the second Alta California leader and founder of Mission Nuestra Señora de la Soledad.

Once at the site, they built a hut and an altar out of sticks and mud.

On October 9, 1791, Fray Lasuén arrived to the site accompanied by soldiers, and the two friars who would run the day-to-day operations of the mission, Fray Diego García and Fray Mariano Rubí. The friars brought with them religious vestments—meaning robes that are worn for special ceremonies—and objects necessary for the founding ceremony. Fray Lasuén placed a cross in the ground and blessed it. Then he said Mass, a

Catholic ceremony celebrating God and Jesus. This ceremony showed that the site was now sacred and belonged to Spain.

Soon after the founding ceremony, Fray Lasuén left the mission, leaving Fray García and Fray Rubí fully in charge. It was then time to build.

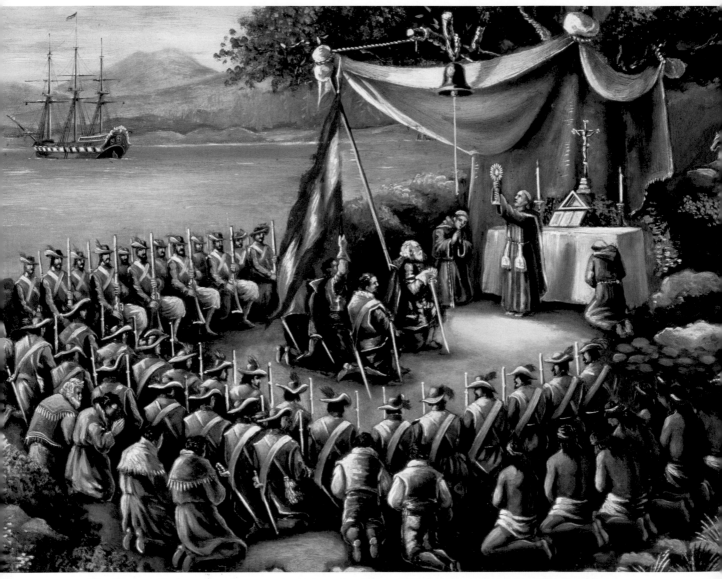

Traditionally, missions were dedicated with a religious ceremony called a Mass, usually said by the president of the missions at that time. This painting from the late nineteenth century depicts Fray Serra performing Mass in Monterey.

5
Early Days at Mission Soledad

After the founding ceremony, there was much work to do. A church had to be built, farming needed to begin, and the missionaries wanted to **baptize** the local Esselen and convert them to Christianity. However, the friars leading the mission did not get along. Fray García was a hard worker, but Fray Rubí preferred to play jokes, pretended to be sick, and complained of mission life. Before long, tensions between the two grew.

STARTING SLOWLY

In Mission Soledad's first year, very little was accomplished. The changing weather conditions made it difficult to work for long periods of time. The bottom of the valley was dry and windy in the summer and cold during the winter. Within the first year, a temporary church was built of wood and covered with a roof made from mud and grass. Livestock—meaning farm animals, such as pigs, cattle, or sheep kept for use or profit—had been brought from other missions, and farming was getting under way.

The friars, however, were having little success with converting the Esselen. By the end of 1792, they had only been able to get eleven Native people to convert to Christianity and live with them at the mission. This was perhaps because the population was so small, and the friars did not know how to speak the language. Also, the Esselen had their own beliefs and were not interested in hearing what the friars had to say or in changing their ways.

Fray Lasuén was not pleased with Fray Rubí, nor was he pleased with Mission Soledad's progress. Fray Lasuén wrote to officials in New Spain requesting that Fray Rubí be allowed to return home. Friars usually had to serve for ten years at the missions before they were allowed to leave. Yet Fray Rubí's behavior and constant pretending to be sick made him an exception. Eventually, after a doctor's note excused Fray Rubí from his duties, he was sent back to Spain and was replaced by Fray Bartolomé Gilí, who after only three years was also removed from the mission in 1794.

MISSION LAYOUT

Each mission's design followed a general layout. Usually they were quadrangular, meaning the buildings were built in a square shape. The important structures, such as the missionaries' living quarters and the church, were in the middle of the square. Outside the square were an orchard and a cemetery. The friars lived separately from the neophyte population. At Mission Soledad, neophytes lived at the south end of the quadrangle, sometimes in buildings that resembled their traditional huts. Girls and unmarried women often lived in *monjeríos*, which are dormitories that would be locked at night. The buildings were made from adobe brick, which was a mixture of dirt, water, and straw that had been formed into a brick shape and hardened in the sun.

Most of the buildings took a long time to finish, but by 1810, all of the mission buildings were complete. There was a chapel, a church, four granaries, offices, a kitchen, living quarters for priests and neophytes, and a guardhouse. Other buildings that shaped the mission into a community included a mill, a shoemaker's shop, and a weaving house. The grounds held a vineyard and an orchard.

THE CHURCH

Progress at Mission Soledad was slow because of all the problems with Fray Rubí and Fray Gilí. Fray García was also unpopular and was said to mistreat the neophytes. Not many neophytes lived at Mission Soledad, and little work was done. Although it took a while, once the temporary wooden church was built, work began on a more permanent adobe church. The few neophytes that were

At all the missions, laborers used adobe bricks to construct the buildings. These bricks were made by hand using nearby resources like mud and straw.

at the mission did most of the work. They made the adobe bricks and constructed the walls of the church. Several adobe churches at the other missions were finished in one to two years, but the church at Mission Nuestra Señora de la Soledad took seven years to complete. The small church was finished at last in 1797.

CROPS

There were several crops that did well at Mission Soledad. These included olives, barley, corn, beans, peas, and the most important to Mission Soledad: wheat.

Many crops grew at Mission Soledad, but wheat was one of the most important.

Crops were grown here because the friars and neophytes built an **aqueduct** that carried water from a river 15 miles (24 km) away to the mission. This meant that the mission had plenty of water for planting as well as drinking, bathing, and nourishing livestock.

LEADERSHIP

Life for the friars, as well as the Native people, was not easy at Mission Soledad. During its existence, the mission went through thirty different leaders, most of whom left after only a year or two of service. This was because of the harsh climate and the few neophytes who joined the mission.

6
Everyday Life

Life for all who lived at Mission Soledad was challenging. Not only did everyone have to deal with new living conditions, they had to follow strict schedules of eating, praying, and working in a new environment. Life for the neophytes who joined the mission proved the most difficult.

When the neophytes lived in their villages—meaning the original communities in which indigenous Americans lived before the arrival of the Spanish—they had been free to hunt and gather, perform their own ceremonies, and do as they chose. At the mission, they had to obey the friars and follow soldiers' orders while they worked. Another event that governed their life was the ringing of the bell, which called them to every activity.

BELLS

Bells were very important to the entire mission system. Each mission had a bell or a series of bells that were rung to alert people living at the mission that a different activity was about to occur. Bells usually rang in the morning, once to notify people of prayer time, and another for breakfast. After breakfast it rang to signal the workday, at midday to call all to lunch, in the evening to stop work for the day, and at night for bed.

The bell at Mission Soledad was made in 1794 and hung from a wooden beam beside the church's entrance. Tied to it was a rope so that the friars could ring it every day. Today the original bell sits in the church, while a replica of the original swings outside the church.

The original mission bell hung outside the church for many years but now sits inside.

THE DAY'S AGENDA

Most days at Mission Soledad began with the ringing of the church bell at 6:00 a.m. Morning prayer lasted a half hour, and breakfast was at 6:30 a.m. The neophytes ate *atole*, a soup made from corn and beans.

After breakfast, it was time for work. The male neophytes did leatherworking and wood crafting as well as farming and blacksmithing. Of particular importance at the missions was the creation of their olive groves. The olive grove at Mission Soledad was the only grove to have been built using mission-era techniques for planting and cultivation. These groves were planted and cared for by the neophytes. Today the grove remains a main feature of the mission heritage site.

The women were responsible for preparing food, weaving, candle making, and soapmaking. They learned how to cook many

Spanish foods, which they prepared for everyone at the mission. The children helped with the work and attended classes, taught by the friars, in Spanish and Bible studies.

At noon the bells rang to call everyone to the midday meal. Lunch consisted of a meat and vegetable stew called *pozole*. It was a good meal, rich in protein, which gave the workers energy. At 1:00 p.m. there was a short rest period called a *siesta*. During this time the neophytes usually prayed or practiced their Spanish or Bible studies, while the friars sometimes preached or rested. Then at 3:00 p.m. siesta was over and everyone returned to work. Evening prayers were scheduled for 5:00 p.m., followed by some free time.

During the free time, the neophytes talked, sang, danced, and played games. However, they could not visit their families in the villages they had left behind, unless granted permission. At the mission, men and women lived separately from one another, although families were usually allowed to stay together. Women were scheduled to go to bed at 8:00 p.m., and men went to bed at 9:00 p.m.

LIVING CONDITIONS

Although the neophytes and priests had buildings to shelter them from the weather, they often had to work outdoors in spite of severe conditions. The weather in the Salinas River Valley could vary from hot to cold to damp. This caused poor living conditions for the people at the mission. One of the reasons many friars left Mission Soledad was because the poor climate led to ill health. Likewise, life for the neophytes was not easy.

Mission Soledad's population size grew more slowly than other missions.

The villages and free lifestyle the neophytes left behind seemed distant. The mission system had brought order and unfamiliar customs to the lives of the neophytes, and before long, many Native people regretted living there. Some tried to escape, and few were successful. Each time they were brought back and were punished.

POPULATION AT MISSION SOLEDAD

Mission Soledad had a rough start in converting the Esselen. But before long, the neophyte population increased. This was because soldiers and friars had made expeditions into other parts of the Monterey area to convert Native people of other tribes and bring them to Mission Soledad—often by force. In the early 1800s, almost 500 neophytes were living at Mission Nuestra Señora de la Soledad. Things seemed to be improving for the mission, but not for long.

7
Success, Hardship, and Decline

The 1800s signaled a new era for Mission Nuestra Señora de la Soledad. Fray García had left in 1797, after serving ten years in the mission system. In the early 1800s, a friar named Antonio Jaymé taught the neophytes how to build an aqueduct that would bring water to the mission. Overall mission population, crop production, and livestock numbers were growing. However, tragedy in many forms soon arose.

DEADLY DISEASES

Mission Soledad had finally begun to thrive, when in 1802, it suffered a terrible setback. An epidemic, thought to be smallpox, swept through the mission, killing many of the Native people living there. Because the converts never had been exposed to European illnesses such as smallpox, they had no way to fight these deadly diseases. This meant most who caught the illness became deathly ill. For a while, an average of six people died each day. The population at the mission decreased even further because neophytes who were not sick ran away to escape the disease. When the epidemic ended, the people at Mission Soledad had

Fray Sarría was a beloved friar at Mission Soledad. After his death, the neophytes carried him to Mission San Antonio de Padua to be buried.

suffered greatly, but they were determined to continue strengthening the mission.

FRAY IBÁÑEZ

In 1803, a friar named Fray Florencio Ibáñez came to Mission Nuestra Señora de la Soledad. Unlike other friars at the mission who often left willingly or were asked to leave, Fray Ibáñez remained at Mission Soledad for fifteen years, until his death in 1818.

Fray Ibáñez worked hard to make Mission Soledad more successful. He wrote plays for the neophytes to perform at religious festivals, called *fiestas*. He was a good manager, and the neophytes liked him better than many of the former friars who passed through the mission.

By 1804, life at Mission Nuestra Señora de la Soledad was going so well that 687 neophytes were living there. Because the population was larger than when the earlier church had been built, Fray Ibáñez decided that the mission needed a new church. Work began in 1808.

VISITORS

On July 24, 1814, an important visitor came to Mission Soledad. A good friend of Fray Ibáñez's, José Joaquín de Arrillaga had become the governor of *Las Californias*, or The Californias. De Arrillaga was in the middle of touring all of the missions when he suddenly became ill. Fray Ibáñez cared for his friend as best he could, but the governor died two days later. He was buried beneath the church floor.

In 1818, a pirate named Hippolyte de Bouchard and his crew attacked the presidio at Monterey Bay. The pirates looted the presidio, taking with them valuable property and destroying items they could not steal. Friars at nearby missions were afraid that Bouchard would soon come after their missions. Mission Soledad was further inland than most of the other missions, so many friars, soldiers, and neophytes traveled there for safety. When the friars heard that de Bouchard had left the area, they returned to their missions. However, before they left, they had to bury Fray Ibáñez, who died on November 26, 1818, at the age of 78.

A friar named Vicente Francisco de Sarría came to live at the mission after Fray Ibáñez died. He had served for six years as the **prefect** of all the California missions. This meant that he worked with the mission president to make sure that all of the friars were performing their religious duties and living in the way that friars should. Fray Sarría had become the mission prefect in 1812, and in 1818, he voluntarily quit his position to work at Mission Soledad.

FLOODS

Because of their location in the Salinas River Valley, floods sometimes occurred at Mission Soledad. In 1824 and 1832, severe flooding damaged the church and the sacristy—a room in a church where sacred objects and garments are kept. The mission buildings were almost entirely ruined. It would be years before the structures were fully restored.

THE NEOPHYTES DEPART

With the mission in such terrible shape, many neophytes began to leave. More left when New Spain, renamed Mexico, won its independence from Spain in 1821 and neophytes were freed from the missions.

With so few neophytes left, there were not enough people there to do all of the work needed to grow crops. Food became scarce, and many of the people at the mission became weak and sick. On Sunday, May 24, 1835, Fray Sarría died while celebrating Mass in the church at Mission Soledad. Many people believe that he died of starvation. The remaining neophytes carried his body to Mission San Antonio de Padua, where he was buried. After Fray Sarría's death, very few neophytes returned to the mission. No more friars were sent to Mission Nuestra Señora de la Soledad.

8
Secularization

Secularization was the process by which control of the missions changed from the Catholic Church to the government. The Spanish friars' version of secularization—handing the missions over to the neophytes to manage after ten years—did not happen because the friars did not believe that the neophytes were ready to assume full responsibility for the missions.

During secularization many Native people left the missions to start new lives as ranch hands for landowners elsewhere.

The Mexican government, now in control of Alta California, had different ideas on secularization. In 1833, they passed the Secularization Act, which enabled the mission system to be dissolved. The mission structures and land, however, would remain and be either sold or managed by soldiers, government officials, or ranchers.

Secularization meant neophytes could leave the mission, return to their villages, or seek work elsewhere. Many neophytes left with hope of finding their tribe or searching for work on the ranches or in the *pueblos*. A small portion of the mission lands was also handed over to the neophytes, but in many instances neophytes were given too few resources to maintain the land, or were bought over

After secularization, Mission Nuestra Señora de la Soledad fell into ruin.

by settlers. Some neophytes even ended up working for the ranchers who had taken their property.

MISSION SOLEDAD IS SECULARIZED

Mission Nuestra Señora de la Soledad was secularized in 1835. Still on the grounds when officials arrived to document what remained at the missions included a vineyard; three *ranchos*, or big farms, at branch missions San Lorenzo, San Vicente, and San Fernando; and livestock that included 3,246 cattle, 2,400 sheep, and 32 horses. Only 172 neophytes remained at the mission.

Sadly, after 1841, little of Mission Nuestra Señora de la Soledad remained. In 1846, the Mexican governor Pio Pico sold Mission Nuestra Señora de la Soledad to a man named Feliciano Soberanes for $800. The land that rightfully belonged to the Native people had been sold out from under them. Soberanes used the mission as a ranch house, and it was later a grocery store and a restaurant before being left to deteriorate for almost 100 years.

THE STATE OF CALIFORNIA

Mexico did not possess Alta California for very long. Soon, American settlers started moving into the area to build homes. They wanted California to become part of the United States. In 1846, the United States went to war with Mexico. In 1848, the United States won the Mexican–American War and California became part of the country. In 1850, California became the thirty-first state. Also in the 1850s, President James Buchanan returned some missions to the Catholic Church.

Today the mission has been restored, but preservation work continues.

MISSION NUESTRA SENORA
DE LA SOLEDAD
FOUNDED OCTOBER 9, 1791
RESTORED OCTOBER 9, 1955

9
The
Mission Today

In the years that followed, more Americans settled in California and took an interest in the local history. They built their homes using similar mission architecture, such as archways and tiled roofs. Over time, this also interested settlers in the history of the missions. Groups along the West Coast joined together to restore the mission chain, including Mission Nuestra Señora de la Soledad.

MISSION SOLEDAD

In 1953, a group of women known as the Native Daughters of the Golden West decided to restore the tiny Mission Soledad. When the restoration began, all that remained were piles of adobe dirt and the front portion of the church. Everything else had been destroyed by weather and neglect. Restoration means working to return something, such as the mission structures, to its original state. They first restored the chapel, which had been destroyed in the 1832 flood, and then the *convento*, or the friars' living quarters.

The group built the chapel to look like the original, but they left the crumbling walls that surrounded the church. When the restoration was complete—the chapel in 1954 and the convento in

1963—the mission was handed over to volunteers who had agreed to maintain it. The ruins of the quadrangle, some of the rooms, and the cemetery were left as monuments to the original mission. What is left of the original Mission Soledad can be seen, alone among the fields and trees, standing quietly as it did so many years ago.

THE MISSION TODAY

Mission Nuestra Señora de la Soledad attracts about 1,000 visitors each month. It is located in part of California's flourishing wine country. Today the people caring for the mission participate in making their own wine as well as olive oil. The olive grove was restored in 2000. Mission Soledad today produces some of the most important olives and olive oil in the country. The convento is now a museum, and the mission grounds themselves are fascinating to explore.

Mission Soledad has also undergone many archaeological digs on its site, beginning in the 1950s to the present day. In 2013, a group of archaeologists called Greenwood and Associates excavated the south and west wings of the church, unearthing old artifacts and some of the oldest parts of the original mission grounds. There are plans to reconstruct the original quadrangle in the next few years.

The journey of Mission Nuestra Señora de la Soledad is one of difficulty, but today it stands as a reminder to all of the vast and varied history of California.

10
Make Your Own Mission Model

To make your own model of Mission Nuestra Señora de la Soledad, you will need:

- corrugated cardboard
- dry lasagna noodles
- glue
- miniature flowers and trees
- paint (reddish brown)
- pencil
- scissors
- Styrofoam
- white paper

DIRECTIONS

Adult supervision is suggested.

Step 1: Cut out a cardboard base measuring 16" × 18" (40.6 × 45.7 cm).

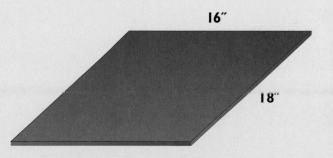

16"

18"

Step 2: Cut out two pieces of Styrofoam measuring 8" × 6" (20.3 × 15.2 cm) each. These will be used to build the front and back church walls.

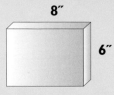

Step 3: Attach the front wall of the church to the base.

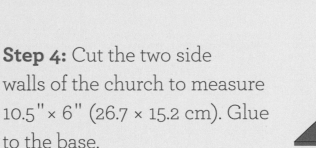

Step 4: Cut the two side walls of the church to measure 10.5" × 6" (26.7 × 15.2 cm). Glue to the base.

Step 5: Take the back wall measuring 8" × 6" (cut out in Step 2), and glue to the base.

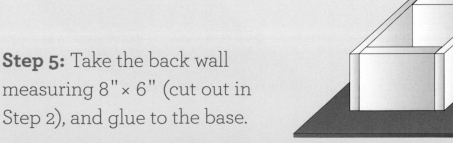

Step 6: Cut out and then glue strips of white paper over the church walls to make them look as if they are covered with plaster.

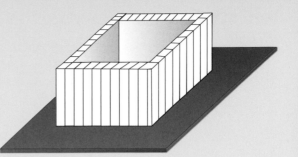

Step 7: To make the front door, draw and then cut out a piece of cardboard measuring 3" × 5" (7.6 × 12.7 cm).

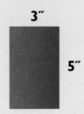

3"

5"

Step 8: Glue the door onto the front of the church.

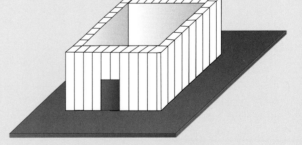

Step 9: To make a roof, cut a piece of cardboard measuring 13" × 11" (33 × 27.9 cm).

13"

11"

Step 10: Fold the cardboard in half, lengthwise, so that the roof will be pointed.

Step 11: To make roof tiles, paint dry lasagna noodles reddish brown. Let them dry.

Step 12: Glue the painted lasagna noodles to the folded cardboard. Let them dry.

Step 13: Glue the roof to the top of the church.

Step 14: Decorate the mission grounds with miniature flowers and trees.

Use this as a reference for building your mission.

Key Dates in Mission History

1492	Christopher Columbus reaches the West Indies
1542	Cabrillo's expedition to California
1602	Sebastian Vizcaíno sails to California
1713	Fray Junípero Serra is born
1769	Founding of San Diego de Alcalá
1770	Founding of San Carlos Borroméo del Río Carmelo
1771	Founding of San Antonio de Padua and San Gabriel Arcángel
1772	Founding of San Luis Obispo de Tolosa
1775–76	Founding of San Juan Capistrano
1776	Founding of San Francisco de Asís
1776	Declaration of Independence is signed

1777	Founding of Santa Clara de Asís
1782	Founding of San Buenaventura
1784	Fray Serra dies
1786	Founding of Santa Bárbara
1787	Founding of La Purísima Concepción
1791	Founding of Santa Cruz and Nuestra Señora de la Soledad
1797	Founding of San José, San Juan Bautista, San Miguel Arcángel, and San Fernando Rey de España
1798	Founding of San Luis Rey de Francia
1804	Founding of Santa Inés
1817	Founding of San Rafael Arcángel
1823	Founding of San Francisco Solano
1849	Gold found in northern California
1850	California becomes the thirty-first state

Glossary

aqueduct (AH-kweh-dukt) A channel or pipe used to carry water, usually for long distances.

baptize (BAP-ty-z) To officially make someone a member of a specified Christian church, the ceremony of baptism is performed. This is usually symbolized by pouring water over someone's head or body, or by immersion.

Catholic (KATH-lik) Someone who believes in the faith or practice of Roman Catholic Christianity, which includes following the spiritual leadership of priests, bishops, and cardinals headed by the pope.

Christianity (kris-chee-A-nih-tee) A religion based on the teachings of Jesus Christ and the Bible, practiced by Eastern, Roman Catholic, and Protestant groups.

convert (kun-VERT) To change from belief in one religion to belief in another religion.

friar (FRY-ur) A brother in a communal religious order. Friars also can be priests.

neophyte (NEE-uh-fyt) What Native Americans were called once they were baptized into the Christian faith.

prefect (PREE-fekt) An administrative official who worked with the mission president to make sure that friars were living and working properly at the missions.

secularization (seh-kyoo-luh-rih-ZAY-shun) When the ownership or control of something is transferred from a religious organization to the state, it is secularized. When the operation of the mission lands was turned over to the neophytes, the process was called secularization.

shamans (SHAH-minz) Medicine men or women who use dancing, singing, and herbs to heal the sick and to control other events in people's lives.

viceroy (VYS-roy) A governor who rules and acts as the representative of the king.

Pronunciation Guide

atole (ah-TOH-lay)

convento (kom-BEN-toh)

El Camino Real (EL kah-MEE-noh RAY-al)

fiestas (fee-EHS-tahs)

monjerío (mohn-hay-REE-oh)

pozole (poh-SOH-lay)

ranchos (RAHN-chohs)

siesta (see-EHS-tah)

soledad (soh-leh-DAD)

Find Out More

To learn more about the California missions, check out these books and websites.

BOOKS

Brower, Pauline. *Inland Valleys Missions of California.* Minneapolis, MN: Lerner Publishing, 2008.

Kalman, Bobbie. *Life of the California Coast Nations.* New York, NY: Crabtree Publications, 2004.

Leffingwell, Randy, and Alastair Worden. *California Missions and Presidios.* St. Paul, MN: Voyageur Press, 2005.

Rocca, Al M. *Esselen & Spanish Courage: A Story of the California Mission Period.* 2nd ed. Seattle, WA: Createspace, 2008.

Weber, Francis J. *Blessed Fray Junípero Serra: An Outstanding California Hero.* Bowling Green, MO: Editions Du Signe, 2008.

Young, Stanley, Melba Levick, and Sally B. Woodbridge. *The Missions of California.* San Francisco, CA: Chronicle Books, 2004.

WEBSITES

California Missions Resource Center

www.missionscalifornia.com

Discover essential facts about each mission and research using the mission timeline and map, photo and illustration gallery, and other resources about each mission.

Esselen Tribe of Monterey County

www.esselen.com

Download a colorful map of the Esselen territory, explore the Esselen language, and learn lots of new words through the English-Esselen dictionary.

Mission Soledad

www.missionsoledad.com

Learn more about Mission Soledad and view large photos of its structure and grounds. Look for updates on the mission's reconstruction and archaeology.

Mission Tour

www.missiontour.org/soledad

Explore all twenty-one missions through a virtual tour filled with photographs, rotating panorama views of the churches, cemeteries, and courtyards.

Index